PASSWORD KEEPER

Copyright 2015

WEBSITE:

Username: _____

Password: _____

Email Linked: _____

Notes: _____

WEBSITE:

Username: _____

Password: _____

Email Linked: _____

Notes: _____

WEBSITE:

Username: _____

Password: _____

Email Linked: _____

Notes: _____

WEBSITE:

Username: _____

Password: _____

Email Linked: _____

Notes: _____

WEBSITE:

Username: _____

Password: _____

Email Linked: _____

Notes: _____

WEBSITE:

Username: _____

Password: _____

Email Linked: _____

Notes: _____

WEBSITE:

Username: _____

Password: _____

Email Linked: _____

Notes: _____

WEBSITE:

Username: _____

Password: _____

Email Linked: _____

Notes: _____

WEBSITE:

Username: _____

Password: _____

Email Linked: _____

Notes: _____

WEBSITE:

Username: _____

Password: _____

Email Linked: _____

Notes: _____

WEBSITE:	WEBSITE:
Username: _____	Username: _____
Password: _____	Password: _____
Email Linked: _____	Email Linked: _____
Notes: _____	Notes: _____

WEBSITE:	WEBSITE:
Username: _____	Username: _____
Password: _____	Password: _____
Email Linked: _____	Email Linked: _____
Notes: _____	Notes: _____

WEBSITE:	WEBSITE:
Username: _____	Username: _____
Password: _____	Password: _____
Email Linked: _____	Email Linked: _____
Notes: _____	Notes: _____

WEBSITE:	WEBSITE:
Username: _____	Username: _____
Password: _____	Password: _____
Email Linked: _____	Email Linked: _____
Notes: _____	Notes: _____

WEBSITE:	WEBSITE:
Username: _____	Username: _____
Password: _____	Password: _____
Email Linked: _____	Email Linked: _____
Notes: _____	Notes: _____

WEBSITE:

Username: _____

Password: _____

Email Linked: _____

Notes: _____

WEBSITE:

Username: _____

Password: _____

Email Linked: _____

Notes: _____

WEBSITE:

Username: _____

Password: _____

Email Linked: _____

Notes: _____

WEBSITE:

Username: _____

Password: _____

Email Linked: _____

Notes: _____

WEBSITE:

Username: _____

Password: _____

Email Linked: _____

Notes: _____

WEBSITE:

Username: _____

Password: _____

Email Linked: _____

Notes: _____

WEBSITE:

Username: _____

Password: _____

Email Linked: _____

Notes: _____

WEBSITE:

Username: _____

Password: _____

Email Linked: _____

Notes: _____

WEBSITE:

Username: _____

Password: _____

Email Linked: _____

Notes: _____

WEBSITE:

Username: _____

Password: _____

Email Linked: _____

Notes: _____

WEBSITE:

Username: _____

Password: _____

Email Linked: _____

Notes: _____

WEBSITE:

Username: _____

Password: _____

Email Linked: _____

Notes: _____

WEBSITE:

Username: _____

Password: _____

Email Linked: _____

Notes: _____

WEBSITE:

Username: _____

Password: _____

Email Linked: _____

Notes: _____

WEBSITE:

Username: _____

Password: _____

Email Linked: _____

Notes: _____

WEBSITE:

Username: _____

Password: _____

Email Linked: _____

Notes: _____

WEBSITE:

Username: _____

Password: _____

Email Linked: _____

Notes: _____

WEBSITE:

Username: _____

Password: _____

Email Linked: _____

Notes: _____

WEBSITE:

Username: _____

Password: _____

Email Linked: _____

Notes: _____

WEBSITE:

Username: _____

Password: _____

Email Linked: _____

Notes: _____

WEBSITE:

Username: _____

Password: _____

Email Linked: _____

Notes: _____

WEBSITE:

Username: _____

Password: _____

Email Linked: _____

Notes: _____

WEBSITE:

Username: _____

Password: _____

Email Linked: _____

Notes: _____

WEBSITE:

Username: _____

Password: _____

Email Linked: _____

Notes: _____

WEBSITE:

Username: _____

Password: _____

Email Linked: _____

Notes: _____

WEBSITE:

Username: _____

Password: _____

Email Linked: _____

Notes: _____

WEBSITE:

Username: _____

Password: _____

Email Linked: _____

Notes: _____

WEBSITE:

Username: _____

Password: _____

Email Linked: _____

Notes: _____

WEBSITE:

Username: _____

Password: _____

Email Linked: _____

Notes: _____

WEBSITE:

Username: _____

Password: _____

Email Linked: _____

Notes: _____

WEBSITE:

Username: _____

Password: _____

Email Linked: _____

Notes: _____

WEBSITE:

Username: _____

Password: _____

Email Linked: _____

Notes: _____

WEBSITE:

Username: _____

Password: _____

Email Linked: _____

Notes: _____

WEBSITE:

Username: _____

Password: _____

Email Linked: _____

Notes: _____

WEBSITE:

Username: _____

Password: _____

Email Linked: _____

Notes: _____

WEBSITE:

Username: _____

Password: _____

Email Linked: _____

Notes: _____

WEBSITE:

Username: _____

Password: _____

Email Linked: _____

Notes: _____

WEBSITE:

Username: _____

Password: _____

Email Linked: _____

Notes: _____

WEBSITE:

Username: _____

Password: _____

Email Linked: _____

Notes: _____

WEBSITE:

Username: _____

Password: _____

Email Linked: _____

Notes: _____

WEBSITE:

Username: _____

Password: _____

Email Linked: _____

Notes: _____

WEBSITE:

Username: _____

Password: _____

Email Linked: _____

Notes: _____

WEBSITE:

Username: _____

Password: _____

Email Linked: _____

Notes: _____

WEBSITE:

Username: _____

Password: _____

Email Linked: _____

Notes: _____

WEBSITE:

Username: _____

Password: _____

Email Linked: _____

Notes: _____

WEBSITE:

Username: _____

Password: _____

Email Linked: _____

Notes: _____

WEBSITE:

Username: _____

Password: _____

Email Linked: _____

Notes: _____

WEBSITE:

Username: _____

Password: _____

Email Linked: _____

Notes: _____

WEBSITE:

Username: _____

Password: _____

Email Linked: _____

Notes: _____

WEBSITE:

Username: _____

Password: _____

Email Linked: _____

Notes: _____

WEBSITE:

Username: _____

Password: _____

Email Linked: _____

Notes: _____

WEBSITE:

Username: _____

Password: _____

Email Linked: _____

Notes: _____

WEBSITE:

Username: _____

Password: _____

Email Linked: _____

Notes: _____

WEBSITE:

Username: _____

Password: _____

Email Linked: _____

Notes: _____

WEBSITE:

Username: _____

Password: _____

Email Linked: _____

Notes: _____

WEBSITE:

Username: _____

Password: _____

Email Linked: _____

Notes: _____

WEBSITE:

Username: _____

Password: _____

Email Linked: _____

Notes: _____

WEBSITE:

Username: _____

Password: _____

Email Linked: _____

Notes: _____

WEBSITE:

Username: _____

Password: _____

Email Linked: _____

Notes: _____

WEBSITE:

Username: _____

Password: _____

Email Linked: _____

Notes: _____

WEBSITE:

Username: _____

Password: _____

Email Linked: _____

Notes: _____

WEBSITE:

Username: _____

Password: _____

Email Linked: _____

Notes: _____

WEBSITE:

Username: _____

Password: _____

Email Linked: _____

Notes: _____

WEBSITE:

Username: _____

Password: _____

Email Linked: _____

Notes: _____

WEBSITE:

Username: _____

Password: _____

Email Linked: _____

Notes: _____

WEBSITE:

Username: _____

Password: _____

Email Linked: _____

Notes: _____

WEBSITE:

Username: _____

Password: _____

Email Linked: _____

Notes: _____

WEBSITE:

Username: _____

Password: _____

Email Linked: _____

Notes: _____

WEBSITE:

Username: _____

Password: _____

Email Linked: _____

Notes: _____

WEBSITE:

Username: _____

Password: _____

Email Linked: _____

Notes: _____

WEBSITE:

Username: _____

Password: _____

Email Linked: _____

Notes: _____

WEBSITE:

Username: _____

Password: _____

Email Linked: _____

Notes: _____

WEBSITE:

Username: _____

Password: _____

Email Linked: _____

Notes: _____

WEBSITE:

Username: _____

Password: _____

Email Linked: _____

Notes: _____

WEBSITE:

Username: _____

Password: _____

Email Linked: _____

Notes: _____

WEBSITE:

Username: _____

Password: _____

Email Linked: _____

Notes: _____

WEBSITE:

Username: _____

Password: _____

Email Linked: _____

Notes: _____

WEBSITE:

Username: _____

Password: _____

Email Linked: _____

Notes: _____

WEBSITE:

Username: _____

Password: _____

Email Linked: _____

Notes: _____

WEBSITE:

Username: _____

Password: _____

Email Linked: _____

Notes: _____

WEBSITE:

Username: _____

Password: _____

Email Linked: _____

Notes: _____

WEBSITE:

Username: _____

Password: _____

Email Linked: _____

Notes: _____

WEBSITE:

Username: _____

Password: _____

Email Linked: _____

Notes: _____

WEBSITE:

Username: _____

Password: _____

Email Linked: _____

Notes: _____

WEBSITE:

Username: _____

Password: _____

Email Linked: _____

Notes: _____

WEBSITE:

Username: _____

Password: _____

Email Linked: _____

Notes: _____

WEBSITE:

Username: _____

Password: _____

Email Linked: _____

Notes: _____

WEBSITE:

Username: _____

Password: _____

Email Linked: _____

Notes: _____

WEBSITE:

Username: _____

Password: _____

Email Linked: _____

Notes: _____

WEBSITE:

Username: _____

Password: _____

Email Linked: _____

Notes: _____

WEBSITE:

Username: _____

Password: _____

Email Linked: _____

Notes: _____

WEBSITE:

Username: _____

Password: _____

Email Linked: _____

Notes: _____

WEBSITE:

Username: _____

Password: _____

Email Linked: _____

Notes: _____

WEBSITE:

Username: _____

Password: _____

Email Linked: _____

Notes: _____

WEBSITE:

Username: _____

Password: _____

Email Linked: _____

Notes: _____

WEBSITE:

Username: _____

Password: _____

Email Linked: _____

Notes: _____

WEBSITE:

Username: _____

Password: _____

Email Linked: _____

Notes: _____

WEBSITE:

Username: _____

Password: _____

Email Linked: _____

Notes: _____

WEBSITE:

Username: _____

Password: _____

Email Linked: _____

Notes: _____

WEBSITE:

Username: _____

Password: _____

Email Linked: _____

Notes: _____

WEBSITE:

Username: _____

Password: _____

Email Linked: _____

Notes: _____

WEBSITE:

Username: _____

Password: _____

Email Linked: _____

Notes: _____

WEBSITE:

Username: _____

Password: _____

Email Linked: _____

Notes: _____

WEBSITE:

Username: _____

Password: _____

Email Linked: _____

Notes: _____

WEBSITE:

Username: _____

Password: _____

Email Linked: _____

Notes: _____

WEBSITE:

Username: _____

Password: _____

Email Linked: _____

Notes: _____

WEBSITE:

Username: _____

Password: _____

Email Linked: _____

Notes: _____

WEBSITE:

Username: _____

Password: _____

Email Linked: _____

Notes: _____

WEBSITE:

Username: _____

Password: _____

Email Linked: _____

Notes: _____

WEBSITE:

Username: _____

Password: _____

Email Linked: _____

Notes: _____

WEBSITE:

Username: _____

Password: _____

Email Linked: _____

Notes: _____

WEBSITE:

Username: _____

Password: _____

Email Linked: _____

Notes: _____

WEBSITE:

Username: _____

Password: _____

Email Linked: _____

Notes: _____

WEBSITE:

Username: _____

Password: _____

Email Linked: _____

Notes: _____

WEBSITE:

Username: _____

Password: _____

Email Linked: _____

Notes: _____

WEBSITE:

Username: _____

Password: _____

Email Linked: _____

Notes: _____

WEBSITE:

Username: _____

Password: _____

Email Linked: _____

Notes: _____

WEBSITE:

Username: _____

Password: _____

Email Linked: _____

Notes: _____

WEBSITE:

Username: _____

Password: _____

Email Linked: _____

Notes: _____

WEBSITE:

Username: _____

Password: _____

Email Linked: _____

Notes: _____

WEBSITE:

Username: _____

Password: _____

Email Linked: _____

Notes: _____

WEBSITE:

Username: _____

Password: _____

Email Linked: _____

Notes: _____

WEBSITE:

Username: _____

Password: _____

Email Linked: _____

Notes: _____

WEBSITE:

Username: _____

Password: _____

Email Linked: _____

Notes: _____

WEBSITE:

Username: _____

Password: _____

Email Linked: _____

Notes: _____

WEBSITE:

Username: _____

Password: _____

Email Linked: _____

Notes: _____

WEBSITE:

Username: _____

Password: _____

Email Linked: _____

Notes: _____

WEBSITE:

Username: _____

Password: _____

Email Linked: _____

Notes: _____

WEBSITE:

Username: _____

Password: _____

Email Linked: _____

Notes: _____

WEBSITE:

Username: _____

Password: _____

Email Linked: _____

Notes: _____

PAGE: _____ OF _____

WEBSITE:

Username: _____

Password: _____

Email Linked: _____

Notes: _____

WEBSITE:

Username: _____

Password: _____

Email Linked: _____

Notes: _____

WEBSITE:

Username: _____

Password: _____

Email Linked: _____

Notes: _____

WEBSITE:

Username: _____

Password: _____

Email Linked: _____

Notes: _____

WEBSITE:

Username: _____

Password: _____

Email Linked: _____

Notes: _____

WEBSITE:

Username: _____

Password: _____

Email Linked: _____

Notes: _____

WEBSITE:

Username: _____

Password: _____

Email Linked: _____

Notes: _____

WEBSITE:

Username: _____

Password: _____

Email Linked: _____

Notes: _____

WEBSITE:

Username: _____

Password: _____

Email Linked: _____

Notes: _____

WEBSITE:

Username: _____

Password: _____

Email Linked: _____

Notes: _____

WEBSITE:

Username: _____

Password: _____

Email Linked: _____

Notes: _____

WEBSITE:

Username: _____

Password: _____

Email Linked: _____

Notes: _____

WEBSITE:

Username: _____

Password: _____

Email Linked: _____

Notes: _____

WEBSITE:

Username: _____

Password: _____

Email Linked: _____

Notes: _____

WEBSITE:

Username: _____

Password: _____

Email Linked: _____

Notes: _____

WEBSITE:

Username: _____

Password: _____

Email Linked: _____

Notes: _____

WEBSITE:

Username: _____

Password: _____

Email Linked: _____

Notes: _____

WEBSITE:

Username: _____

Password: _____

Email Linked: _____

Notes: _____

WEBSITE:

Username: _____

Password: _____

Email Linked: _____

Notes: _____

WEBSITE:

Username: _____

Password: _____

Email Linked: _____

Notes: _____

WEBSITE:
Username: _____
Password: _____
Email Linked: _____
Notes: _____

WEBSITE:
Username: _____
Password: _____
Email Linked: _____
Notes: _____

WEBSITE:
Username: _____
Password: _____
Email Linked: _____
Notes: _____

WEBSITE:
Username: _____
Password: _____
Email Linked: _____
Notes: _____

WEBSITE:
Username: _____
Password: _____
Email Linked: _____
Notes: _____

WEBSITE:
Username: _____
Password: _____
Email Linked: _____
Notes: _____

WEBSITE:
Username: _____
Password: _____
Email Linked: _____
Notes: _____

WEBSITE:
Username: _____
Password: _____
Email Linked: _____
Notes: _____

WEBSITE:
Username: _____
Password: _____
Email Linked: _____
Notes: _____

WEBSITE:
Username: _____
Password: _____
Email Linked: _____
Notes: _____

WEBSITE:

Username: _____

Password: _____

Email Linked: _____

Notes: _____

WEBSITE:

Username: _____

Password: _____

Email Linked: _____

Notes: _____

WEBSITE:

Username: _____

Password: _____

Email Linked: _____

Notes: _____

WEBSITE:

Username: _____

Password: _____

Email Linked: _____

Notes: _____

WEBSITE:

Username: _____

Password: _____

Email Linked: _____

Notes: _____

WEBSITE:

Username: _____

Password: _____

Email Linked: _____

Notes: _____

WEBSITE:

Username: _____

Password: _____

Email Linked: _____

Notes: _____

WEBSITE:

Username: _____

Password: _____

Email Linked: _____

Notes: _____

WEBSITE:

Username: _____

Password: _____

Email Linked: _____

Notes: _____

WEBSITE:

Username: _____

Password: _____

Email Linked: _____

Notes: _____

WEBSITE:

Username: _____

Password: _____

Email Linked: _____

Notes: _____

WEBSITE:

Username: _____

Password: _____

Email Linked: _____

Notes: _____

WEBSITE:

Username: _____

Password: _____

Email Linked: _____

Notes: _____

WEBSITE:

Username: _____

Password: _____

Email Linked: _____

Notes: _____

WEBSITE:

Username: _____

Password: _____

Email Linked: _____

Notes: _____

WEBSITE:

Username: _____

Password: _____

Email Linked: _____

Notes: _____

WEBSITE:

Username: _____

Password: _____

Email Linked: _____

Notes: _____

WEBSITE:

Username: _____

Password: _____

Email Linked: _____

Notes: _____

WEBSITE:

Username: _____

Password: _____

Email Linked: _____

Notes: _____

WEBSITE:

Username: _____

Password: _____

Email Linked: _____

Notes: _____

WEBSITE:

Username: _____

Password: _____

Email Linked: _____

Notes: _____

WEBSITE:

Username: _____

Password: _____

Email Linked: _____

Notes: _____

WEBSITE:

Username: _____

Password: _____

Email Linked: _____

Notes: _____

WEBSITE:

Username: _____

Password: _____

Email Linked: _____

Notes: _____

WEBSITE:

Username: _____

Password: _____

Email Linked: _____

Notes: _____

WEBSITE:

Username: _____

Password: _____

Email Linked: _____

Notes: _____

WEBSITE:

Username: _____

Password: _____

Email Linked: _____

Notes: _____

WEBSITE:

Username: _____

Password: _____

Email Linked: _____

Notes: _____

WEBSITE:

Username: _____

Password: _____

Email Linked: _____

Notes: _____

WEBSITE:

Username: _____

Password: _____

Email Linked: _____

Notes: _____

PAGE: _____ OF _____

WEBSITE:

Username: _____

Password: _____

Email Linked: _____

Notes: _____

WEBSITE:

Username: _____

Password: _____

Email Linked: _____

Notes: _____

WEBSITE:

Username: _____

Password: _____

Email Linked: _____

Notes: _____

WEBSITE:

Username: _____

Password: _____

Email Linked: _____

Notes: _____

WEBSITE:

Username: _____

Password: _____

Email Linked: _____

Notes: _____

WEBSITE:

Username: _____

Password: _____

Email Linked: _____

Notes: _____

WEBSITE:

Username: _____

Password: _____

Email Linked: _____

Notes: _____

WEBSITE:

Username: _____

Password: _____

Email Linked: _____

Notes: _____

WEBSITE:

Username: _____

Password: _____

Email Linked: _____

Notes: _____

WEBSITE:

Username: _____

Password: _____

Email Linked: _____

Notes: _____

WEBSITE:

Username: _____

Password: _____

Email Linked: _____

Notes: _____

WEBSITE:

Username: _____

Password: _____

Email Linked: _____

Notes: _____

WEBSITE:

Username: _____

Password: _____

Email Linked: _____

Notes: _____

WEBSITE:

Username: _____

Password: _____

Email Linked: _____

Notes: _____

WEBSITE:

Username: _____

Password: _____

Email Linked: _____

Notes: _____

WEBSITE:

Username: _____

Password: _____

Email Linked: _____

Notes: _____

WEBSITE:

Username: _____

Password: _____

Email Linked: _____

Notes: _____

WEBSITE:

Username: _____

Password: _____

Email Linked: _____

Notes: _____

WEBSITE:

Username: _____

Password: _____

Email Linked: _____

Notes: _____

WEBSITE:

Username: _____

Password: _____

Email Linked: _____

Notes: _____

WEBSITE:
Username: _____
Password: _____
Email Linked: _____
Notes: _____

WEBSITE:
Username: _____
Password: _____
Email Linked: _____
Notes: _____

WEBSITE:
Username: _____
Password: _____
Email Linked: _____
Notes: _____

WEBSITE:
Username: _____
Password: _____
Email Linked: _____
Notes: _____

WEBSITE:
Username: _____
Password: _____
Email Linked: _____
Notes: _____

WEBSITE:
Username: _____
Password: _____
Email Linked: _____
Notes: _____

WEBSITE:
Username: _____
Password: _____
Email Linked: _____
Notes: _____

WEBSITE:
Username: _____
Password: _____
Email Linked: _____
Notes: _____

WEBSITE:
Username: _____
Password: _____
Email Linked: _____
Notes: _____

WEBSITE:
Username: _____
Password: _____
Email Linked: _____
Notes: _____

WEBSITE:

Username: _____

Password: _____

Email Linked: _____

Notes: _____

WEBSITE:

Username: _____

Password: _____

Email Linked: _____

Notes: _____

WEBSITE:

Username: _____

Password: _____

Email Linked: _____

Notes: _____

WEBSITE:

Username: _____

Password: _____

Email Linked: _____

Notes: _____

WEBSITE:

Username: _____

Password: _____

Email Linked: _____

Notes: _____

WEBSITE:

Username: _____

Password: _____

Email Linked: _____

Notes: _____

WEBSITE:

Username: _____

Password: _____

Email Linked: _____

Notes: _____

WEBSITE:

Username: _____

Password: _____

Email Linked: _____

Notes: _____

WEBSITE:

Username: _____

Password: _____

Email Linked: _____

Notes: _____

WEBSITE:

Username: _____

Password: _____

Email Linked: _____

Notes: _____

WEBSITE:	WEBSITE:
Username: _____	Username: _____
Password: _____	Password: _____
Email Linked: _____	Email Linked: _____
Notes: _____	Notes: _____

WEBSITE:	WEBSITE:
Username: _____	Username: _____
Password: _____	Password: _____
Email Linked: _____	Email Linked: _____
Notes: _____	Notes: _____

WEBSITE:	WEBSITE:
Username: _____	Username: _____
Password: _____	Password: _____
Email Linked: _____	Email Linked: _____
Notes: _____	Notes: _____

WEBSITE:	WEBSITE:
Username: _____	Username: _____
Password: _____	Password: _____
Email Linked: _____	Email Linked: _____
Notes: _____	Notes: _____

WEBSITE:	WEBSITE:
Username: _____	Username: _____
Password: _____	Password: _____
Email Linked: _____	Email Linked: _____
Notes: _____	Notes: _____

WEBSITE:

Username: _____

Password: _____

Email Linked: _____

Notes: _____

WEBSITE:

Username: _____

Password: _____

Email Linked: _____

Notes: _____

WEBSITE:

Username: _____

Password: _____

Email Linked: _____

Notes: _____

WEBSITE:

Username: _____

Password: _____

Email Linked: _____

Notes: _____

WEBSITE:

Username: _____

Password: _____

Email Linked: _____

Notes: _____

WEBSITE:

Username: _____

Password: _____

Email Linked: _____

Notes: _____

WEBSITE:

Username: _____

Password: _____

Email Linked: _____

Notes: _____

WEBSITE:

Username: _____

Password: _____

Email Linked: _____

Notes: _____

WEBSITE:

Username: _____

Password: _____

Email Linked: _____

Notes: _____

WEBSITE:

Username: _____

Password: _____

Email Linked: _____

Notes: _____

WEBSITE:

Username: _____

Password: _____

Email Linked: _____

Notes: _____

WEBSITE:

Username: _____

Password: _____

Email Linked: _____

Notes: _____

WEBSITE:

Username: _____

Password: _____

Email Linked: _____

Notes: _____

WEBSITE:

Username: _____

Password: _____

Email Linked: _____

Notes: _____

WEBSITE:

Username: _____

Password: _____

Email Linked: _____

Notes: _____

WEBSITE:

Username: _____

Password: _____

Email Linked: _____

Notes: _____

WEBSITE:

Username: _____

Password: _____

Email Linked: _____

Notes: _____

WEBSITE:

Username: _____

Password: _____

Email Linked: _____

Notes: _____

WEBSITE:

Username: _____

Password: _____

Email Linked: _____

Notes: _____

WEBSITE:

Username: _____

Password: _____

Email Linked: _____

Notes: _____

PAGE: _____ OF _____

WEBSITE:

Username: _____

Password: _____

Email Linked: _____

Notes: _____

WEBSITE:

Username: _____

Password: _____

Email Linked: _____

Notes: _____

WEBSITE:

Username: _____

Password: _____

Email Linked: _____

Notes: _____

WEBSITE:

Username: _____

Password: _____

Email Linked: _____

Notes: _____

WEBSITE:

Username: _____

Password: _____

Email Linked: _____

Notes: _____

WEBSITE:

Username: _____

Password: _____

Email Linked: _____

Notes: _____

WEBSITE:

Username: _____

Password: _____

Email Linked: _____

Notes: _____

WEBSITE:

Username: _____

Password: _____

Email Linked: _____

Notes: _____

WEBSITE:

Username: _____

Password: _____

Email Linked: _____

Notes: _____

WEBSITE:

Username: _____

Password: _____

Email Linked: _____

Notes: _____

WEBSITE:	WEBSITE:
Username: _____	Username: _____
Password: _____	Password: _____
Email Linked: _____	Email Linked: _____
Notes: _____	Notes: _____

WEBSITE:	WEBSITE:
Username: _____	Username: _____
Password: _____	Password: _____
Email Linked: _____	Email Linked: _____
Notes: _____	Notes: _____

WEBSITE:	WEBSITE:
Username: _____	Username: _____
Password: _____	Password: _____
Email Linked: _____	Email Linked: _____
Notes: _____	Notes: _____

WEBSITE:	WEBSITE:
Username: _____	Username: _____
Password: _____	Password: _____
Email Linked: _____	Email Linked: _____
Notes: _____	Notes: _____

WEBSITE:	WEBSITE:
Username: _____	Username: _____
Password: _____	Password: _____
Email Linked: _____	Email Linked: _____
Notes: _____	Notes: _____

WEBSITE:

Username: _____

Password: _____

Email Linked: _____

Notes: _____

WEBSITE:

Username: _____

Password: _____

Email Linked: _____

Notes: _____

WEBSITE:

Username: _____

Password: _____

Email Linked: _____

Notes: _____

WEBSITE:

Username: _____

Password: _____

Email Linked: _____

Notes: _____

WEBSITE:

Username: _____

Password: _____

Email Linked: _____

Notes: _____

WEBSITE:

Username: _____

Password: _____

Email Linked: _____

Notes: _____

WEBSITE:

Username: _____

Password: _____

Email Linked: _____

Notes: _____

WEBSITE:

Username: _____

Password: _____

Email Linked: _____

Notes: _____

WEBSITE:

Username: _____

Password: _____

Email Linked: _____

Notes: _____

WEBSITE:

Username: _____

Password: _____

Email Linked: _____

Notes: _____

WEBSITE:

Username: _____

Password: _____

Email Linked: _____

Notes: _____

WEBSITE:

Username: _____

Password: _____

Email Linked: _____

Notes: _____

WEBSITE:

Username: _____

Password: _____

Email Linked: _____

Notes: _____

WEBSITE:

Username: _____

Password: _____

Email Linked: _____

Notes: _____

WEBSITE:

Username: _____

Password: _____

Email Linked: _____

Notes: _____

WEBSITE:

Username: _____

Password: _____

Email Linked: _____

Notes: _____

WEBSITE:

Username: _____

Password: _____

Email Linked: _____

Notes: _____

WEBSITE:

Username: _____

Password: _____

Email Linked: _____

Notes: _____

WEBSITE:

Username: _____

Password: _____

Email Linked: _____

Notes: _____

WEBSITE:

Username: _____

Password: _____

Email Linked: _____

Notes: _____

PAGE: _____ OF _____

WEBSITE:

Username: _____

Password: _____

Email Linked: _____

Notes: _____

WEBSITE:

Username: _____

Password: _____

Email Linked: _____

Notes: _____

WEBSITE:

Username: _____

Password: _____

Email Linked: _____

Notes: _____

WEBSITE:

Username: _____

Password: _____

Email Linked: _____

Notes: _____

WEBSITE:

Username: _____

Password: _____

Email Linked: _____

Notes: _____

WEBSITE:

Username: _____

Password: _____

Email Linked: _____

Notes: _____

WEBSITE:

Username: _____

Password: _____

Email Linked: _____

Notes: _____

WEBSITE:

Username: _____

Password: _____

Email Linked: _____

Notes: _____

WEBSITE:

Username: _____

Password: _____

Email Linked: _____

Notes: _____

WEBSITE:

Username: _____

Password: _____

Email Linked: _____

Notes: _____

WEBSITE:	WEBSITE:
Username: _____	Username: _____
Password: _____	Password: _____
Email Linked: _____	Email Linked: _____
Notes:_____	Notes:_____

WEBSITE:	WEBSITE:
Username: _____	Username: _____
Password: _____	Password: _____
Email Linked: _____	Email Linked: _____
Notes:_____	Notes:_____

WEBSITE:	WEBSITE:
Username: _____	Username: _____
Password: _____	Password: _____
Email Linked: _____	Email Linked: _____
Notes:_____	Notes:_____

WEBSITE:	WEBSITE:
Username: _____	Username: _____
Password: _____	Password: _____
Email Linked: _____	Email Linked: _____
Notes:_____	Notes:_____

WEBSITE:	WEBSITE:
Username: _____	Username: _____
Password: _____	Password: _____
Email Linked: _____	Email Linked: _____
Notes:_____	Notes:_____

WEBSITE:

Username: _____

Password: _____

Email Linked: _____

Notes: _____

WEBSITE:

Username: _____

Password: _____

Email Linked: _____

Notes: _____

WEBSITE:

Username: _____

Password: _____

Email Linked: _____

Notes: _____

WEBSITE:

Username: _____

Password: _____

Email Linked: _____

Notes: _____

WEBSITE:

Username: _____

Password: _____

Email Linked: _____

Notes: _____

WEBSITE:

Username: _____

Password: _____

Email Linked: _____

Notes: _____

WEBSITE:

Username: _____

Password: _____

Email Linked: _____

Notes: _____

WEBSITE:

Username: _____

Password: _____

Email Linked: _____

Notes: _____

WEBSITE:

Username: _____

Password: _____

Email Linked: _____

Notes: _____

WEBSITE:

Username: _____

Password: _____

Email Linked: _____

Notes: _____

WEBSITE:	WEBSITE:
Username: _____	Username: _____
Password: _____	Password: _____
Email Linked: _____	Email Linked: _____
Notes: _____	Notes: _____

WEBSITE:	WEBSITE:
Username: _____	Username: _____
Password: _____	Password: _____
Email Linked: _____	Email Linked: _____
Notes: _____	Notes: _____

WEBSITE:	WEBSITE:
Username: _____	Username: _____
Password: _____	Password: _____
Email Linked: _____	Email Linked: _____
Notes: _____	Notes: _____

WEBSITE:	WEBSITE:
Username: _____	Username: _____
Password: _____	Password: _____
Email Linked: _____	Email Linked: _____
Notes: _____	Notes: _____

WEBSITE:	WEBSITE:
Username: _____	Username: _____
Password: _____	Password: _____
Email Linked: _____	Email Linked: _____
Notes: _____	Notes: _____

WEBSITE:

Username: _____

Password: _____

Email Linked: _____

Notes: _____

WEBSITE:

Username: _____

Password: _____

Email Linked: _____

Notes: _____

WEBSITE:

Username: _____

Password: _____

Email Linked: _____

Notes: _____

WEBSITE:

Username: _____

Password: _____

Email Linked: _____

Notes: _____

WEBSITE:

Username: _____

Password: _____

Email Linked: _____

Notes: _____

WEBSITE:

Username: _____

Password: _____

Email Linked: _____

Notes: _____

WEBSITE:

Username: _____

Password: _____

Email Linked: _____

Notes: _____

WEBSITE:

Username: _____

Password: _____

Email Linked: _____

Notes: _____

WEBSITE:

Username: _____

Password: _____

Email Linked: _____

Notes: _____

WEBSITE:

Username: _____

Password: _____

Email Linked: _____

Notes: _____

PAGE: _____ OF _____

WEBSITE:

Username: _____

Password: _____

Email Linked: _____

Notes: _____

WEBSITE:

Username: _____

Password: _____

Email Linked: _____

Notes: _____

WEBSITE:

Username: _____

Password: _____

Email Linked: _____

Notes: _____

WEBSITE:

Username: _____

Password: _____

Email Linked: _____

Notes: _____

WEBSITE:

Username: _____

Password: _____

Email Linked: _____

Notes: _____

WEBSITE:

Username: _____

Password: _____

Email Linked: _____

Notes: _____

WEBSITE:

Username: _____

Password: _____

Email Linked: _____

Notes: _____

WEBSITE:

Username: _____

Password: _____

Email Linked: _____

Notes: _____

WEBSITE:

Username: _____

Password: _____

Email Linked: _____

Notes: _____

WEBSITE:

Username: _____

Password: _____

Email Linked: _____

Notes: _____

WEBSITE:

Username: _____

Password: _____

Email Linked: _____

Notes: _____

WEBSITE:

Username: _____

Password: _____

Email Linked: _____

Notes: _____

WEBSITE:

Username: _____

Password: _____

Email Linked: _____

Notes: _____

WEBSITE:

Username: _____

Password: _____

Email Linked: _____

Notes: _____

WEBSITE:

Username: _____

Password: _____

Email Linked: _____

Notes: _____

WEBSITE:

Username: _____

Password: _____

Email Linked: _____

Notes: _____

WEBSITE:

Username: _____

Password: _____

Email Linked: _____

Notes: _____

WEBSITE:

Username: _____

Password: _____

Email Linked: _____

Notes: _____

WEBSITE:

Username: _____

Password: _____

Email Linked: _____

Notes: _____

WEBSITE:

Username: _____

Password: _____

Email Linked: _____

Notes: _____

PAGE: _____ OF _____

WEBSITE:

Username: _____

Password: _____

Email Linked: _____

Notes: _____

WEBSITE:

Username: _____

Password: _____

Email Linked: _____

Notes: _____

WEBSITE:

Username: _____

Password: _____

Email Linked: _____

Notes: _____

WEBSITE:

Username: _____

Password: _____

Email Linked: _____

Notes: _____

WEBSITE:

Username: _____

Password: _____

Email Linked: _____

Notes: _____

WEBSITE:

Username: _____

Password: _____

Email Linked: _____

Notes: _____

WEBSITE:

Username: _____

Password: _____

Email Linked: _____

Notes: _____

WEBSITE:

Username: _____

Password: _____

Email Linked: _____

Notes: _____

WEBSITE:

Username: _____

Password: _____

Email Linked: _____

Notes: _____

WEBSITE:

Username: _____

Password: _____

Email Linked: _____

Notes: _____

WEBSITE:

Username: _____

Password: _____

Email Linked: _____

Notes: _____

WEBSITE:

Username: _____

Password: _____

Email Linked: _____

Notes: _____

WEBSITE:

Username: _____

Password: _____

Email Linked: _____

Notes: _____

WEBSITE:

Username: _____

Password: _____

Email Linked: _____

Notes: _____

WEBSITE:

Username: _____

Password: _____

Email Linked: _____

Notes: _____

WEBSITE:

Username: _____

Password: _____

Email Linked: _____

Notes: _____

WEBSITE:

Username: _____

Password: _____

Email Linked: _____

Notes: _____

WEBSITE:

Username: _____

Password: _____

Email Linked: _____

Notes: _____

WEBSITE:

Username: _____

Password: _____

Email Linked: _____

Notes: _____

WEBSITE:

Username: _____

Password: _____

Email Linked: _____

Notes: _____

PAGE: _____ OF _____

WEBSITE:

Username: _____

Password: _____

Email Linked: _____

Notes: _____

WEBSITE:

Username: _____

Password: _____

Email Linked: _____

Notes: _____

WEBSITE:

Username: _____

Password: _____

Email Linked: _____

Notes: _____

WEBSITE:

Username: _____

Password: _____

Email Linked: _____

Notes: _____

WEBSITE:

Username: _____

Password: _____

Email Linked: _____

Notes: _____

WEBSITE:

Username: _____

Password: _____

Email Linked: _____

Notes: _____

WEBSITE:

Username: _____

Password: _____

Email Linked: _____

Notes: _____

WEBSITE:

Username: _____

Password: _____

Email Linked: _____

Notes: _____

WEBSITE:

Username: _____

Password: _____

Email Linked: _____

Notes: _____

WEBSITE:

Username: _____

Password: _____

Email Linked: _____

Notes: _____

WEBSITE:

Username: _____

Password: _____

Email Linked: _____

Notes: _____

WEBSITE:

Username: _____

Password: _____

Email Linked: _____

Notes: _____

WEBSITE:

Username: _____

Password: _____

Email Linked: _____

Notes: _____

WEBSITE:

Username: _____

Password: _____

Email Linked: _____

Notes: _____

WEBSITE:

Username: _____

Password: _____

Email Linked: _____

Notes: _____

WEBSITE:

Username: _____

Password: _____

Email Linked: _____

Notes: _____

WEBSITE:

Username: _____

Password: _____

Email Linked: _____

Notes: _____

WEBSITE:

Username: _____

Password: _____

Email Linked: _____

Notes: _____

WEBSITE:

Username: _____

Password: _____

Email Linked: _____

Notes: _____

WEBSITE:

Username: _____

Password: _____

Email Linked: _____

Notes: _____

WEBSITE:

Username: _____

Password: _____

Email Linked: _____

Notes: _____

WEBSITE:

Username: _____

Password: _____

Email Linked: _____

Notes: _____

WEBSITE:

Username: _____

Password: _____

Email Linked: _____

Notes: _____

WEBSITE:

Username: _____

Password: _____

Email Linked: _____

Notes: _____

WEBSITE:

Username: _____

Password: _____

Email Linked: _____

Notes: _____

WEBSITE:

Username: _____

Password: _____

Email Linked: _____

Notes: _____

WEBSITE:

Username: _____

Password: _____

Email Linked: _____

Notes: _____

WEBSITE:

Username: _____

Password: _____

Email Linked: _____

Notes: _____

WEBSITE:

Username: _____

Password: _____

Email Linked: _____

Notes: _____

WEBSITE:

Username: _____

Password: _____

Email Linked: _____

Notes: _____

PAGE: _____ OF _____

WEBSITE:

Username: _____

Password: _____

Email Linked: _____

Notes: _____

WEBSITE:

Username: _____

Password: _____

Email Linked: _____

Notes: _____

WEBSITE:

Username: _____

Password: _____

Email Linked: _____

Notes: _____

WEBSITE:

Username: _____

Password: _____

Email Linked: _____

Notes: _____

WEBSITE:

Username: _____

Password: _____

Email Linked: _____

Notes: _____

WEBSITE:

Username: _____

Password: _____

Email Linked: _____

Notes: _____

WEBSITE:

Username: _____

Password: _____

Email Linked: _____

Notes: _____

WEBSITE:

Username: _____

Password: _____

Email Linked: _____

Notes: _____

WEBSITE:

Username: _____

Password: _____

Email Linked: _____

Notes: _____

WEBSITE:

Username: _____

Password: _____

Email Linked: _____

Notes: _____

PAGE: _____ OF _____

WEBSITE:	WEBSITE:
Username: _____	Username: _____
Password: _____	Password: _____
Email Linked: _____	Email Linked: _____
Notes:_____	Notes:_____

WEBSITE:	WEBSITE:
Username: _____	Username: _____
Password: _____	Password: _____
Email Linked: _____	Email Linked: _____
Notes:_____	Notes:_____

WEBSITE:	WEBSITE:
Username: _____	Username: _____
Password: _____	Password: _____
Email Linked: _____	Email Linked: _____
Notes:_____	Notes:_____

WEBSITE:	WEBSITE:
Username: _____	Username: _____
Password: _____	Password: _____
Email Linked: _____	Email Linked: _____
Notes:_____	Notes:_____

WEBSITE:	WEBSITE:
Username: _____	Username: _____
Password: _____	Password: _____
Email Linked: _____	Email Linked: _____
Notes:_____	Notes:_____

PAGE: _____ OF _____

WEBSITE:

Username: _____

Password: _____

Email Linked: _____

Notes: _____

WEBSITE:

Username: _____

Password: _____

Email Linked: _____

Notes: _____

WEBSITE:

Username: _____

Password: _____

Email Linked: _____

Notes: _____

WEBSITE:

Username: _____

Password: _____

Email Linked: _____

Notes: _____

WEBSITE:

Username: _____

Password: _____

Email Linked: _____

Notes: _____

WEBSITE:

Username: _____

Password: _____

Email Linked: _____

Notes: _____

WEBSITE:

Username: _____

Password: _____

Email Linked: _____

Notes: _____

WEBSITE:

Username: _____

Password: _____

Email Linked: _____

Notes: _____

WEBSITE:

Username: _____

Password: _____

Email Linked: _____

Notes: _____

WEBSITE:

Username: _____

Password: _____

Email Linked: _____

Notes: _____

WEBSITE:

Username: _____

Password: _____

Email Linked: _____

Notes: _____

WEBSITE:

Username: _____

Password: _____

Email Linked: _____

Notes: _____

WEBSITE:

Username: _____

Password: _____

Email Linked: _____

Notes: _____

WEBSITE:

Username: _____

Password: _____

Email Linked: _____

Notes: _____

WEBSITE:

Username: _____

Password: _____

Email Linked: _____

Notes: _____

WEBSITE:

Username: _____

Password: _____

Email Linked: _____

Notes: _____

WEBSITE:

Username: _____

Password: _____

Email Linked: _____

Notes: _____

WEBSITE:

Username: _____

Password: _____

Email Linked: _____

Notes: _____

WEBSITE:

Username: _____

Password: _____

Email Linked: _____

Notes: _____

WEBSITE:

Username: _____

Password: _____

Email Linked: _____

Notes: _____

PAGE: _____ OF _____